To Sarah,
Thought this might have some useful tips in it, even if you don't make it back to actual running.

Love Kerry xx

# A RUNNERS GUIDE

# TO HEALING LOW BACK INJURY

**ERIN KANOA**

First Published in 2012

© Copyright 2012 by Erin Kanoa

All rights reserved. No part of this publication may be reproduced or distributed in any form or by any means, electronic or mechanical, or stored in a database or retrieval system, without prior written permission from the publisher.

This book is for educational purposes. The publisher and author of this instructional book are not responsible in any manner whatsoever for any adverse effects arising directly or indirectly as a result of the information provided in this book. If not practiced safely and with caution, exercise can be dangerous to you and others.

The ideas, concepts, and opinions expressed in this book should be used for educational purposes only. This book is sold with the understanding that the author and publisher are not rendering medical advice of any kind, nor is this book intended to replace medical advice, nor to diagnose, prescribe or treat any disease, condition, illness, or injury.

Before beginning any exercise program, including any guidance in this book, it is imperative that you receive full medical clearance from a licensed physician. The author and publisher claim no responsibility to any person or entity for any liability, loss, or damage caused or alleged to be caused directly or indirectly as a result of the use, application, or interpretation of the material in this book.

# DEDICATION

*To Simone and Carmen:*
*Your inspiration and love*
*are with me always!*

*And to my running buddy Schatzi,*
*for the love only a dog can give.*

# Contents

Acknowledgements i

About the Author ii

Introduction 1

Understanding the Cause of Your Low Back Injury 2

Sleuthing Your Low Back Injury 6

How Do I Get Out of Here ? 14

What to Do While Recovering 23

How to Choose Your Recovery Team 28

Special Topics 31

The First Run Back 41

Conclusion 47

## Acknowledgements

The adage "it takes a village", doesn't just apply to raising children; it can also apply to healing from an injury. In my case, I assembled a village of professionals, friends, and coworkers and would like to acknowledge some of them here with the thought that you can assemble a similar team.

I would first like to thank my intuitive healer and chiropractor, Dr. Lindon Keeler, DC, and his wonderful staff, for their commitment to the highest quality, full body-mind chiropractic care; Elizabeth Hampton, physical therapist and owner of Core PT, for her amazing knowledge of the core muscles of the body and her enthusiasm in teaching clients how to harness that power for a stronger body; Juliana Bohn, an amazing structural therapist, who understands the subtle essence of the spine; the amazingly knowledgeable massage therapists at Advanced Medical Massage Group, for giving me weekly care and sculpting a better me - one massage at a time; Susan Bradbury, for being a compassionate and spiritual acupuncturist; Dr. Park, LAC, for helping me realign my body's energy meridians; my best friend, Lauren Heine, for her constant compassion and support during the rough times; and my friend, Shannon Wright, for running slow with me on those first days and having it not matter! And to the fabulous running community of Bellingham, WA - specifically the crew at Fairhaven Runners - I love you all!

## About the Author

For much of her life, Erin Kanoa has been an active and competitive athlete. Beginning in her early thirties she trained as an ultra-marathoner, as well as a pre-Olympic biathlete. Through various injuries, specifically back injuries, she has had to crawl her way back to fitness—sometimes literally crawl! And yes, she continues to be an avid runner.

She was a neuromuscular massage therapist through her mid-twenties, with a focus on injury treatment and working with athletes. She also taught massage for several years during that time, giving her a full understanding of the body from a biomechanical and holistic healing perspective. Since then, she has been an energy engineer and visual effects artist in the movie industry, excelling in analysis and digital art design solutions. Erin continues to enjoy her passion of running trails and competing in local trail running races.

www.erinkanoa.com

Look for her next books , *Running Comfortably in your 40's* and *Athletic to Pathetic: A Runners Guide to Burnout Recovery*!

# Introduction

*A back injury is the body's way of asking for*
*whole body & mind healing*
Erin Kanoa

I was inspired to write this book after successfully healing several low-back injuries the past few years - a bulged disc three years ago; and a bilateral fracture to my L5 vertebrae a year after that. The medical consensus on the fracture was that it would take a year or more to get back to running, with possible pain for many years to come. In four months however, I was running pain-free and stronger than ever!

The speedy recovery from the fracture was possible by applying all I had learned about recovery up until that point; while working with a competent team of physical therapists, an excellent chiropractor, private Pilates instructors, weekly therapeutic massage, gradual, healthy weight loss, a revised and improved diet, and changing a pretty stressful life. Addressing those components simultaneously is what allowed me to heal my low back so quickly.

This book will cover the various aspects of healing of your injury - through self-reflective questions and example stories, and provide a recovery plan, designed to help all injured athletes, specifically runners, get back to running as soon as possible!

# Understanding the Cause of Your Low-Back Injury

If your back injury does not have an obvious cause (such as a fall), you might be asking yourself, "How the &!!%?! did I get here???" Knowing how you got injured is paramount to your recovery. Not only do you want to heal from the pain, you want to prevent getting injured again. It's about you and your unique healing process. It may take some time and sleuthing on your part, but that's okay; you probably have more time on your hands right now. You may be staring at the ceiling, laying awake at night due to pain, or working your way through that second bag of chips—yikes! Use this upsetting time to reflect on how you got here. Spend 10 percent of your time on reflection and 90 percent on the solution. A few days of wallowing is okay, it will get you grounded in your sad, painful state. It will show you where you are starting from. But that is all it is - your starting point. It's all about getting better from here on out!

**Types of Back Injuries**

After reading numerous journals and books, asking a lot of questions, and engaging many qualified professionals, I realized that back injuries are complex and unique to the individual. However, they all follow certain trends, which means that they can be avoided or at least healed more quickly, when proper measures are taken.

In my experience there are two types of back injuries: multi-micro trauma and massive trauma. Multi-micro traumas sneak up on you. They are the ones where the slightest move one day creates a painful misalignment. Massive trauma injuries are caused by a car accident, a fall, improper lifting, or some obviously single traumatic event. The sneaky ones beg the question, "How did this happen???" In those situations, you may ask yourself that very question hundreds of times.

To understand the sneaky style injuries, we must get a better understanding of what the back does. The back is designed to bear the burden of a lot of physical and emotional stress. It carries the weight of the body while upright and provides core structure while laying down. In times of emotional stress, our postural muscles absorb that tension.

Our back is happiest when the musculoskeletal framework is balanced (the muscles are not too tight in one area or weak in another). However, over time, the body can become imbalanced, causing muscle fibers to not fire neural impulses properly. At this point, an injury can be caused by the slightest action - like picking up a five-hundred-pound sock while getting dressed! The sock wasn't five hundred pounds, but it might as well have been.

We get injured, and we blame the sock. Most people have stories like this: "I was getting out of the car; petting the dog, and I blew out my back!" You can injure your back by picking up a sock, but this is merely the last insult in a long string of micro injuries and imbalance. This is how the body shows its tipping point and gets your attention.

In the story below, I share the circumstances of my first ever sneaky back injury in my early twenties - to show that injuries of this nature should really not be a surprise.

**Run-In with a Sacroiliac Injury**

The Setup: I had always been athletic — track and field, basketball, swimming, cycling, mountain biking, downhill and slalom skiing, and snowboarding—doing it all with a little bit of crazy and a lot of heart. This was coupled with years of not stretching or doing any restorative activities other than watching movies or walks on the beach. So, it shouldn't have been a surprise that day, when a debilitating spasm in my sacroiliac (SI) joint erupted from just picking up a sock!

At the time, I was in college, and had just finished an intense forty-five minute session on the rowing machine, jumped in the shower, got out to get dressed for classes, reached down to the laundry basket to grab a pair of socks, and BAM! The next second, I hit the floor, writhing in such agony that I had to drag the phone off the counter by the cord to call for help. This low-back injury was no accident—it was imminent! My body had become totally imbalanced, my mother had been diagnosed as terminally ill, I had just ended a relationship, and was working overtime to keep up with my heavy course load. The trifecta of stress was going on: physical, emotional, and mental. Back then, I didn't understand that posture, muscle balance, and spiritual health were all factors in an injury.

My mind was in a whirl: how did I get here? As I reflected, it all started to make sense: Being an avid cyclist after a decade of daily cycling, who never stretched, created "butt lock." That is, my butt was hard as a rock—and as a result of that over tightness, it was screwing up the balance of my low back!

After a few years of on and off pain, it got better, but was a winding road and just the beginning of fully understanding the complex nature of low-back pain. During that time I started yoga, getting regular massage, trail running as cross-training and exploring how the body works. The point to make here, is that some habits were changed, and produced okay results, but it was not a comprehensive approach to healing.

## SLEUTHING YOUR LOW-BACK INJURY

*"Your life can only be as free as your perception of it"*
Deepak Chopra

In order to heal more quickly, I have found it helps to understand the circumstances of your injury and take a current status report of ones life, which can take time. In an effort to speed up that process, I have consolidated the following list of questions that helped me recover more quickly than ever.

### LOW BACK REFLECTION QUESTIONS

**1. What is your current stress level?** Do you hate your job? How is your relationship? Have you had a death in the family? Assess how you are feeling in your life circumstance.

**2. How frequently do you run? Do you cross-train?**

**3. Do you understand what core stability is?** Core typically refers to the group of abdominal muscles that are closest to the spine which provide proper posture and movement.

**4. Do you have a regular Pilates or yoga practice?**

**5. How restful is your sleep?**

6. How is your diet? How healthy do you eat?

7. Are you overweight?

8. Do you "overdo it" in running and in life? Do you workout too much? Do you build recovery time into your workout regime?

9. Are you a "weekend warrior" when it comes to exercise?

10. How much downtime do you have? Do you ever relax?

11. How much time do you spend driving each week? Do you drive a stick shift car?

12. Do you know how to lift from your core?

13. Do you understand general ergonomics and workstation ergonomics?

14. Do you have a biomechanical issue that needs attention?

15. How much water do you drink?

Grab a pen and paper, and write down your answers. If you don't know some of the answers, try your best to find them. Write everything down. I have answered these questions in the following chapter to give you an idea of what to be looking for.

In my experience, all of these topics can contribute to a back injury. Even if your injury was the result of a trauma, these areas will need your attention for the healing process. Your answers to these questions will show you where you need to focus your energy. When you find out how certain areas in your life need changing, you can make adjustments to get your low back feeling great.

**Fresh Injury?**

If you have injured your back today, this is what I suggest you do:

1. Ice the area 10 minutes at a time, with 30 minutes in between, as much as you can, for the first forty-eight hours! Take Zyflammend (A natural turmeric based anti-inflammatory supplement through New Chapter) and Arnica (a plant that helps with sprains and strains) and rest. Topical application of Arnica and Traumeel cream are recommended also.

2. Get a lumbar (low back) support brace at a medical supply store.
3. Assemble your healing team and start making appointments. Find the best physical therapist and chiropractor that you can, as well as a competent injury

treatment massage therapist and acupuncturist.

4. Identify your replacement workouts in lieu of daily running.

5. Get a calorie armband, such as one from BodyMedia - and watch those calories!

6. Get a chin up bar and mount it in a place it can stay.

I cannot emphasize enough the importance of a lumbar support brace during this time. It will ease the pressure on your low back, giving you relief from pain while offering support. It will be important to wear it during exercise and, of course, during your transition to running. It's a short-term fix while your back is returning to balance.
In the story below, I share the athletic woes of my back fracture to show that healing is a process, and knowing your body is an important part of that recovery journey.

**The Story of My Fracture**

While out on a trail run, I landed very, very hard on my backside, after an off-leash dog with errant owners took me out from behind – clipping! Shock and anger washed over me. Tweedle Dee and Tweedle Dummer just stared and had very little to say. (A word of caution here- get their number if this happens to you – I didn't think it was a big deal at the time, turns out it was). Stung and stunned, I finished my run anyway, too proud and having such a fabulous time, determined to persevere. That evening, after dinner and a shower, my lower back started to feel "different" - not sharply painful like my bulged disc of a year ago, thank GOD, but stiff. I figured I had just bruised the area, as my hip was starting to get some color. I shrugged it off; I had no sharp pain, so I was good, yeah?

I still had standing appointments with my physical therapist. At our next appointment she said, "You were lucky. You have no sharp pain, you are walking okay, your muscles test well. Take it easy for a few days, and you should be okay - but we will keep an eye on it." Taking her advice, I took a few days off from running. I was on an every-other-day running cycle, so no harm there. As the weeks progressed though, the stiff feeling began to radiate outward, a sensation not experienced before. My massage therapist checked it out. She said all my muscles were splinting in that area (becoming tight so as to lock down the area of instability) and that gentle stretching, heat, and cold would probably help. It was still feeling about the same after a couple of days of this approach, so I began running again anyway. I ran with my SI brace and was doing okay - no disc pain but more of a weird radiating pressure. I had run through worse pain, I figured it would go away in time. At my next appointment with my PT, she assessed me again – and was starting to get nervous. She asked me to take it easy for a longer stretch and cut out the running. It had been about three weeks after the fall and getting ready to do a few back-to-back business trips, so flying was in my future, the curse of all low-back pain sufferers.

The first trip was more about fun with a little business, did a few runs and felt a little more stiff - "same old, same old" at that point. The second trip was to the East Coast, which meant more time on a plane and in a hotel. I was going crazy for some intense exercise. The hotel had a treadmill, so I started with a slow, easy run. Telling myself that I would chill out at an eleven-minute pace and watch Oprah. Then a young man got on the treadmill next to me, he did his warm up, and then he started running at a decent pace. It was like a greyhound watching the rabbit, I could not stop myself. I picked up the pace, and began pacing him and felt the joy rush over me. Running at a decent pace, ahh, it felt so great!

It was all great for a few minutes, then, as if watching a movie of myself, the room started to get blurry, and it felt like my upper body was drifting away from my lower body. The legs grew weak, rubbery and tingly, and I grew faint and dizzy. Something was seriously wrong. My head started to spin. I had a hard time getting off the treadmill - I had to will my legs to move - they felt tingly like little fairies were dancing inside of them. The fainting feeling grew stronger as I weaved my way toward the elevator. I made my way to my room, grabbed some ice from the fridge (I had brought ice packs with me) and collapsed on the bed. Endorphins rushed though my body like never before. My legs were still tingling, but it was almost euphoric – because I was not on my feet anymore. I felt giddy in my panic and shivered uncontrollably, even though I was hot and sweaty. What was going on?? I speed dialed my physical therapist, and described what was going on, she said to apply ice, keep the SI brace on 24/7 , and get on the first plane back home. I was in disbelief. She said, "I think your back is broken or fractured, and the bones have slid forward compressing your spinal cord. Lay down as much as you can. We'll need to x-ray you ASAP!!"

My reality took a huge shift into the Twilight Zone - hello??!? spinal cord !?? In addition to the SI brace, I had tied a jacket as tight as I could around my waist - which gave more support to the lumbar area. By the time I got off the plane, I could not stand for more than a minute at a time before my legs gave out. It was a very vulnerable and scary place to be, and the x-ray confirmed that she was right – bilateral L5 displaced fracture. The prescription was bed rest for two weeks with a lumbar corset brace. This meant crawling around the house to bathe and get to the kitchen. The requirement was to wear the brace 24/7 and I was looking down a road of uncertainty regarding my future in running and a possible surgery. It was all about how well it would heal the doctor said. It was all up to me, and there were no guarantees. If it didn't heal well, they would have to cut and put pins in my vertebrae and possibly lose bladder control function given the area of spinal cord impingement. Ugh… I had seen a friends back push out her pins from a vertebral fusion surgery, and I was not going to wear a diaper the rest of my life - these were not options for me! So…I focused.

My recovery started with getting grounded with my circumstances. I already had a great healing team from the bulged disc. I saw my PT twice a week after bed rest was over. During the bed rest time I began arm presses and using the chin up bar to hang and pull up from, to get gentle traction on my spine. Arm presses were done all day - this was my only outlet! I took 3x the prescribed amount of Zyflammend and amazingly was able to take no pain killers as a result! A few short moments of breath taking pain ensued if I moved just the wrong way, but overall my pain was kept bearable. Natural topical analgesics were used constantly and I rested. A non-inflammatory diet was started and I upped my mineral intake - to support my bones knitting. Making homemade bone broth soups are highly recommended.

It took about 2 months before normal sitting resumed. Otherwise, I had to lay down or be very extended in the car for car rides. Driving myself was out of the question. I worked with my team, and they helped me heal. It felt like a long process, but only took about 3 months. At that time, I was ready to have the brace off during the night. So for 3 months the corset was worn 24/7 and I contemplated where my life was going. At the end of month 4, the time had come. I took off the brace, went for a glorious treadmill run - and it was so amazing!

## How Do I Get Out of Here?

*"If your sense of self is expanded, it experiences a relaxed body and a friendly, open environment where your intentions synchronistically fulfill themselves"*
Deepak Chopra

Let's review the list of fifteen questions from the last chapter, and I will describe how I answered the questions for myself and made the needed changes in my life to heal my back.

### 1. What is my current stress level?

We all have life issues that come up, and you currently might be wading through a string of challenges, but the *backdrop* of your life should be low stress. If it's not, make moves to getting it there. Stress reduction is one of the core tenants in chronic pain management. Numerous studies cite the correlation between stress and pain, stress and disease. The byproducts of chronic stress are real, and they will set up your body for injury. Symptoms may include headaches, muscle tightness, weight gain, insomnia, decreased recovery from exercise and eventual burnout. You may need to change your job, spouse, or living situation to de-stress, but in the long run, you will be healthier. Make time for yourself, create a yoga practice or other activities that brighten your spirit. Stress is about perception, you have to find what is relaxing for you.

## 2. How frequently do you run? Do you cross-train?

Running is awesome, but cross-training makes your running even better. Cycling, elliptical training, swimming, skate skiing, yoga, Pilates, strength training, and kickboxing are all great activities to combine with running. It makes sense to have an overall strong and balanced body. Resistance exercises such as strength training and cycling help build muscle and initiate the growth hormone response. This, in combination with cardio-focused workouts is a rocking combo for overall strength improvement and therefore injury prevention. All elite athletes harness muscle confusion techniques, known as plyometrics, to keep the body growing and expose imbalance: you can too! Activities done on the BOSU ball and other core-demanding work push the body to adapt. Adaptive strengthening is a bulwark against imbalance and promotes the health of the spine.

## 3. Do you understand what core stability is?

Pilates helped me better understand core stability. When your body is working from its core, all movements are more fluid and take less effort. You harness the true ergonomic muscular strength that your body evolved with. For some people, their core is "hooked up," or fully engaged and supporting their daily activities. But for most of us, and especially those with a low-back injury, chances are that your core needs awareness and strengthening. A few personalized sessions with a Pilates instructor is a great way to start. You can then take group classes as you feel comfortable with your form and abilities.

Why Pilates? This is a body toning , core body awareness training that can whip you in to shape fast! I was introduced to Pilates while training for the Olympics. Combine this with muscle-confusion training and a little Ashtanga Yoga, and you have a ticket for increased strength and agility.

## 4. Do you have a regular Pilates or yoga practice?

Commit to a consistent yoga or Pilates practice at least be a few times a week, balanced with other exercises. I have found at least some daily yoga to work miracles on every front.

## 5. How well do you sleep?

Get as much sleep as you can! When I was training for the Olympics, I trained, ate, and slept, and then did it all over again. Sleep is regenerative and will heal you. It can also de-stress you and help your mind work better. In addition, it can help you lose excess weight, as the hormones generated by lack of sleep cause our bodies to retain fat. In general, modern society is sleep deprived. This is partly due to lifestyle, over lit homes, over electronic activities and because we don't sleep in a pitch-black environment (which promotes quality sleep). Get at least eight hours each night, in as dark a room as possible. Get a natural light wake up clock if you have to get up before you naturally would.

### 6. How is your diet?

Eating well means eating healthy foods, preferably Organic, with enough protein, proper fats, and veggies and fruits. It means very little, if any sugar and prepackaged crap. Whole, raw, and properly cooked food will nourish you. Shop at your local farmers market, get local organic meat and vegetables, source healthy oils from avocados, olives, hemp and flaxseed. Chemicals, pesticides, refined sugars and preservatives have no place in a healthy diet.

### 7. Are you overweight?

I am talking more than ten pounds. Even being ten pounds overweight can make a difference in the way you carry yourself. It's easy to put on a few pounds during an injury. When the length of injury is months or longer though, the pounds can add up. If you are already overweight use this time to refocus and drop a few pounds. A lot of people are of the mindset that exercise is the only way to lose weight. Diet is the other half of that equation, and even with minimal low impact or no exercise you can still lose weight or maintain your current weight. During my recovery I changed my diet to a more lower calorie, lower carbohydrate, primal style diet -

after all without burning all the calories from daily running, I certainly didn't need the extra carbs!

**8. Do you "overdo" both in running and in life? Do you workout too much? Do you build recovery time into your workout regime?**

The ideal way to harness stress is to take a break from it. There was a book in the late 90's that described how to "stress" for "success". Here's how it works: provide stress for a certain amount of time to initiate growth, then take a break and let that growth happen. It is much the same way as building muscle with weight lifting. The recipe is to lift (tearing microfibers of muscle) then rest. It is during the rest period that the fibers actually heal and build back stronger. If that rest period doesn't happen, the muscle fibers will not heal adequately, leaving the area vulnerable to injury. This same approach works for your life also. Stress, then rest. You will build up endurance after each rest period. Stress, and not rest, and you will burn out and be prone to life injury.

**9. Are you a "weekend warrior" when it comes to exercise?**

Being a "weekend warrior" sets you up for injury, and the ideal is a regimen of daily exercise. No matter how brief, regular exercise is a *must* for proper body conditioning. It's better to run ten minutes each day than an hour on the weekend. Doing both of course is ideal!

## 10. How much downtime do you have? Do you ever relax?

Taking a long lunch or a "no-agenda" walk or talk is rare in our culture. Make it part of your life. Relaxation promotes healthy balance in our body systems. The biochemical's that flood our body when we are relaxed help all systems become more balanced. When we are feeling uptight, our bodies are reflecting this state through high blood pressure, tightening of muscles, increased cortisol and other stress hormones. All of which slowly break down our bodies in addition to our spirits.

## 11. How much time do you spend driving each week? Do you drive a stick shift?

The bane of modern times is the commute! The more you drive, the greater your risk of low-back issues - because sitting in that position shortens the quads (the front muscles of your legs) for long periods of time, setting up the potential for imbalance. In a nutshell, your hamstrings and your quads should ideally be in balance tension wise, so that your hips, and therefore your low back, will not be forced into a chronic position of imbalance. Shifting in traffic is especially hard on the low back, because one hip is working and tense while the other is not, which also causes imbalance. This is where daily yoga, gentle lunges and Pilates come in! The best option is to have a car with a triptronic or an automatic transmission, in addition to the self care. I switched to triptronic and my back is much happier!

## 12. Do you know how to lift from your core?

Bend your knees when you lift! Get your butt under you! We have all heard these instructions , but they can be hard to remember - so practice. I practiced: taking groceries out of the back of my car with an empty grocery bag. I would set my body with a no weight target and practice lifting from the back of my car. When picking things up from off the floor, the golf lift is a godsend. The "golf lift" is when you swing your straight leg back from your hip as you bend down - its often seen when picking up golf balls from the green.

## 13. Do you understand general ergonomics and workstation ergonomics?

If you spend hours at a computer, like I do, be sure you are ergonomically supported. Get the right chair, desk height, low back support, and eye line with your monitor. Personally, I invested in some Herman Miller Aeron chairs. They are the most ergonomically adjustable, comfortable chairs you will find, and will last forever! Yes, they are pricey, but if you spend many hours a day - (in my case 8 or more) then it is beyond worth it. At the end of my day I am pain free and ready to play! I also invested in a standing station set up and go back and forth from a standing station to a sitting station. This really is not too much to ask for yourself or from your company.

## 14. Do you have a biomechanical issue that needs tending to?

While training for the Summer Biathlon National Championships, I tore my right quadratus lumborum during a trail sprint training. I had already warmed up but had hit a slight rock in the trail at near full speed, and pop! Muscle pulled from bone. After not healing for a while, I sought out Paul St. John, the neuromuscular guru in Florida to find the cause of tearing only 1 quad muscle which is highly unusual – usually both leg muscles will tear. In other words, why was this leg more prone to tearing than the other? He took me through a biomechanical assessment and x-ray. Turned out I had a slight length discrepancy. My left femur was short or my right femur was long, depending how you looked at at. Either way, it was determined that I needed to have my left shoes lifted. This would even out my legs while walking or running, thereby lessening the stress on my right leg, the one that had the torn muscle. Even though I went to him because of my torn leg muscle, it was clear that the leg length difference was also contributing to my intermittent back issues. The moment this was corrected, years of pain evaporated and I increased my running speed almost overnight. I am sharing this example because there is always a reason people have chronic pain. And often times it is our job to ultimately find out what is causing it. Correcting that lifelong imbalance helped my low back, my neck etc.. You may need this level of investigation also.

## 15. How much water do you drink?

Running can be very dehydrating. Eating grains and processed foods can also be dehydrating. Drink as much water as you can, but be sure to take minerals as part of your supplement regimen. I add trace minerals to my water to make it stick and make it more valuable to my body. When minerals are present in water, the body is hydrated more effectively that with just straight $H_2O$. In general, you want to take in 8 glasses x 8 ounces of water daily, but you may need more. The body's discs and joints are highly dependent on fluid. I spring for coconut water these days also - great electrolytes and some natural sweetness make it a tasty all around natural running drink - just be sure its pure coconut water without any additives. Non-caffeinated herbal teas are also a great way to hydrate and give you some natural healing benefits at the same time. You can also make your water special but adding fruit slices or berries to naturally flavor it!

## What to Do While Recovering

*"You have the power to turn positive to negative and vice versa"*
Deepak Chopra

As with most things, this recovery time can be whatever you make it - inspiring or depressing. Here are some general guidelines to follow during your recovery.

**Alternate your exercise.**
Commit to other forms of exercise—don't stop running and do nothing. Ask your physical therapist or whomever you are working with for an alternative. Swimming is awesome; if you have access to a pool, swim! The elliptical machine was my drug of choice - it was like running but without the impact. Commit now to reduce your stress and maintain your fitness while you plot your return to running. If your injury is grave and acute, you may be unable to exercise for a while. When I was in that situation, I did arm presses, pull-ups, and strange Thera-band exercises. I got creative, and did everything I could that was pain-free.

**Maintain the strength you have.**
Pilates is a wonderful way to keep or gain core strength, as the key to a strong back is your core! Get a list of Pilates exercises that you can do and do them! Do push-ups and pull-ups, and use upper body weights as your pain allows. Do lat pulls on the machine and standing cables pulls. Focus your pent-up

energy on getting stronger. I ended up doing a lot of hanging chin-up exercises and arm presses, because traction on the spine felt great. If being overweight was a factor in your injury, consider it a wake-up call, and commit to getting a handle on it. Change your diet now! Carrying extra weight is hard on the body, especially the low back. If your weight isn't muscle that is working for you, it is fat that is working against you. Do whatever it takes to adapt your calories to your current burn level. I recommend getting the Bodymedia body bug or some other calorie-burn data collector device that will help you with weight loss.

**Decrease your stress.**
Stress plays a huge role in how the body functions day to day. The mind produces tangible results in the body - think of taking a bite out of a lemon wedge. Your mouth just watered, didn't it? Stress affects the tension levels in the body. Most people hold tension in their legs, gluteal muscles, back, shoulders and neck. Over time, chronic stress compounds postural or injury weakness, so to fully recover from an injury, stress must be addressed. If you are like me, you run to reduce stress! You must find other ways to reduce stress; even better, find the root cause. You might need to quit the terrible job or leave the unsupportive girlfriend or the abusive boyfriend. Help yourself in this way, and your back will love you more.

**Eat really, really healthy.**
Consider doing some light days of cleansing on broths and

teas. Go Organic! We are what we eat, so if you have a good nutrition plan, stick with it. If not, now is an excellent time to make a change. I'll get on my soap box and say go gluten free and, if possible, play around with a Paleo diet, as I think it is the healthiest. Gluten is an inflammatory substance found in wheat and wheat derivatives, and it plays a role in your back injury, I guarantee you. Dairy and soy, in many cases, are no better inflammation wise, so try eliminating them from your diet, and see how you feel. You may even consider going all out and do the GAPS Intro diet - the diet that heals your gut, and as a result helps heal food allergies.

**Invest in a rebounder.**
This is a mini-trampoline - start playing with gentle bouncing as your pain levels allow.

**Get plenty of rest and sleep.**
Chances are that your sleep is being disrupted by pain or worry. You need rest, but can't get it. Make the changes that will promote deep sleep. This could look like; sleeping by yourself, taking herbal sleep aides and pain relievers, and taking naps when you feel tired. Make restful sleep a priority, as rebuilding occurs while we sleep. Do not skip this step, make it a priority!

**Honor where you are at.**
For example, the back fracture was a mind bender - it took tons of patience and focus to just walk again, let alone run.

The first hurdle, was saving my spinal cord from permanent damage - so immobilization was necessary. My physician put the fear of God into me when he said, "You have a chance of losing bowl and bladder control should the cord be further disrupted." I became the best immobilized patient ever! If this is where you are at, then really honor that - it will not last forever. Be the best at where you are at, don't try and skip steps - be patient and you will heal.

**Set recovery goals for yourself.**
This could be a timeline of what your milestones are and what you will be doing at each one. I include a sample set of goals below.

**EXAMPLE: Bulged Disc Recovery Goals**
1. To be pain free.
2. To increase range of motion (no more walking and moving like a stiff person).
3. To return to normal activities (picking up things like groceries).
4. To return to athletic activities like walking and hiking.
5. To run again!

Make your own list, and become obsessed with it! Let it consume you. You are healing yourself. A solid support team and a plan help, but only you can make it all happen. Fully commit to your recovery!

## Suggested Reading

*Healing Back Pain , The Mind Body Prescription , The Divided Mind*
Dr. John Sarno
http://www.healingbackpain.com/

*Quantum Healing, Perfect Health*
Deepak Chopra
http://www.deepakchopra.com/

*Lore of Running*
Tim Noakes, MD

*Nourishing Traditions, The Fourfold Path to Healing: Working with the Laws of Nutrition, Therapeutics, Movement and Meditation in the Art of Medicine*
Sally Fallon

*Paleo Diet for Athletes*
Loren Cordain, Ph.D
http://thepaleodiet.com/store/the-paleo-diet-for-athletes

*The Primal Blueprint*
Mark Sisson
http://primalblueprint.com/pages/Mark-Sisson.html

*Gut and Psychology Syndrome*
Natasha Campbell-McBride
http://www.gapsdiet.com/

# How to Choose Your Recovery Team

### Characteristics of a Solid Physical Therapist
Find a physical therapist through referrals from friends, someone who has a proven track record. You will know that you have found a good physical therapist if you are getting results and feel like your questions are being answered. I have heard many people say, "I'm seeing a physical therapist, but I am not getting better." In that case, either the therapist is not working with you where your body is at, or you are not doing the work - meaning, you are not doing the homework that is usually given with the physical therapy session. That "work" might very well be taking it easy for the moment.

> 1. They have a track record of excellent results with other clients.
> 2. Are comfortable with the subtle action of the back and pelvis.
> 3. Communicate and teach you about core strengthening.
> 4. Take their time.

### Characteristics of a Solid Chiropractor
A chiropractor will help your body realign itself. Good chiropractors are knowledgeable about all aspects of the body. Just because they are trained to treat only the spine doesn't mean that they shouldn't be aware of other aspects that affect healing of the body. I find that muscle testing, herbal testing,

and laser therapy are part of an excellent chiropractor's arsenal. They also don't work in a vacuum and should help you build your team with massage therapy, physical therapy and nutrition. The majority of the adjustments should be subtle and not violent. Not all chiropractors are the same, just like not all physical therapists, massage therapists, or physicians are the same. Step up and demand results. If something doesn't feel right with your chiropractic treatment, check it out. The body is designed to heal itself, and you should see steady progress.

**Characteristics of a Solid Massage Therapist**

Personal preferences factor heavily when it comes to massage therapy, but here are some things to look for in a therapeutically trained massage therapist. They will do a postural assessment before they begin to work on you. They will explain how to unwind and rebalance your body. And if you have no imbalances (rare), identify how you are splinting your injury and how to support that process. They help you to make a plan of action based on what they find.

> 1. They work with opposites - if you have back pain, they assess the anterior of your body for over tightening. A good therapist does not work just one part of your back, they "surround the dragon." In other words, the injured area needs attention, yes, but the areas around the injury, that are now overcompensating with tightness, will also need massage.

2. They use a hot compress to soften surrounding muscles and ice after the treatment to minimize inflammation.

3. They are well trained in neuromuscular work or deep tissue work.

4. At times, the treatment may be uncomfortable, but they will help you breathe through the adhesions and other areas of tightness. This will ultimately give way to subtle muscle spasm release and restore blood flow to the area, thereby promoting faster healing, as blood brings needed oxygen to the muscles.

5. Look for a massage therapist who focuses on injury treatment. If you can't find someone in your area, go to someone who can at least ease tension as you heal. Your body will be splinting, and you will need relief from that.

## Special Topics

**Alternative Therapies**

I used an alternative medicine based approach to heal my injuries. I did not seek vertebral fusion, steroids, or cortisone shots. I was interested in understanding why my injury happened and healing it naturally. I have several friends, including world-class runners, who went the vertebral fusion route, and they were happy for the most part at the outset, but as the years progressed (and only a few I might add), they regretted their decision, as they began to feel chronic pain. Why? The reason is simple: joints move. When you take movement out of one joint in your spine through fusion, the other areas of the spine must compensate for the lack of movement. This causes more stress and over movement on the surrounding joints and musculature. It's possible that what you need is a fusion, discectomy, cortisone shots, and other radical procedures, but in most cases with healthy, athletic people, this is not the case. When I speak of alternatives, I mean massage therapy, physical therapy, postural awareness, ergonomics, a healthy diet, a healthy weight, herbal supplements, acupuncture, and safe, enlightened chiropractic —as well as emotional awareness of how you use your body and your stress levels.

**Anatomically Short Legs or Uneven Pelvis**

Some back issues are the culmination of an undiagnosed short leg or uneven pelvis. These conditions are real, subtle, and often overlooked. To uncover them, you must have a leg or pelvis measurement confirmed with x-ray by a professional who knows how to measure. Work with a neuromuscular therapist who understands the complexities of uneven legs to get more information on this. I found out over a decade ago that I have a slightly anatomically short left leg (only 6mm), which can wreak havoc on your back, neck, and SI joint. I now wear a lifted shoe and can stand and run for hours without pain.

## Give Rest to the Restless Mind: Setting Up a Back-to-Running Timeline

One thing that drove me nuts when I was first injured was not knowing how long the healing process would take. The ambiguity was killing me. I started asking for dates, length of time for this and that, and where I should be in terms of pain, Range of Motion (ROM), and fitness. With the help of my physical therapist, I set short-term and long-term goals. No one has a magical crystal ball to answer questions about healing, and everyone's journey is different, but I learned to focus on each goal through to completion. I got a sense of the journey ahead - it would be measured in months.

## "Insanity Management"

If you are like most runners, you need your running! Believe me, I know! You will find yourself climbing the walls and your personality changing. The craziness needs an outlet (don't do what I did initially: overeat!). You can go for it on an elliptical machine, but as far as being outside, that is a tougher problem. You must manage your insanity, or it will undo everything else you do. You'll be doing great and then have a moment of insanity and undo weeks, if not months, of work. Have a substitute outlet in place, something that will help you burn off the crazy "I gotta run" energy. I eventually got into Wii Boxing, going to the gym and some adrenaline hobbies I had set aside. You have to replace your obsession if that is where you are at.

**Unsupportive Relationships**

If you are suffering in an unsupportive relationship, get out of it! Now is the time. You may be injured, but if your relationship is not helping you, it is time to move on! It might sound cliché, but are you "breaking your back" for the relationship? In my case, I realized I was, and it took literally breaking my back to understand the amount of stress I was living with. Sure it was an injury from a fall but a little uncanny. It's worth it to take a good look at your relationship and ask yourself, "Hey, am I happy? Am I feeling supported? Or is it time to move on?"

**Depression Management**

It's depressing to not be able to run. I don't know about you, but running with my dog on the trails is my all-time favorite activity, and when I lost that, it was depressing. Be proactive. Take steps to create buffers and solutions and avoid the slippery slope of being bummed-out. I focused on hobbies I had not made time for, started projects that kept me busy, and hung out with friends who were not runners that I didn't see as often. Find a miniseries, watch movies and read books - fill the space, or trust me, it will be filled by things you don't want.

**Bike Riding**
Some people with low-back injuries can ride a bicycle, but with lumbar injuries, this works only on a case-by-case basis. Extending forward over the bars can exacerbate the disc by placing too much pressure on the front of your body. For me, being an avid cyclist was one of the reasons that my disc bulged in the first place. Sitting crouched over in a tightened pose created an imbalance that set me up for a bulged disc. So if you can be more upright it could work for you - jut approach this one cautiously as it shortens your quads which is typically a bad, bad thing for the low back.

**Pain Management**
Most runners I know, myself included, can tolerate a lot of pain. It takes a high pain tolerance to run long distances and compete at higher levels. Even if you are an easy-going runner who is just staying fit, there is a place where the body requires a certain level of endurance. This state requires focus, and focus is part of your pain-management skill set. This skill serves you with every run, but it can be a disservice when healing. During healing, you are trying to go back to a state where you had no pain. "Pushing through" pain is not what

your body needs. Listen to the subtle cues that your body is giving you.

Managing pain during this time is paramount. Typically, pain is associated with inflammation. In the natural healing and progressive medical community, it is becoming common knowledge that chronic inflammation is the root of most disease in the body. I have learned that if you have unhealthy inflammation from any source—be it related to an injury or diet—healing cannot occur successfully. You must manage the inflammation to remain healthy. A popular route for inflammation management are non-steroidal anti inflammatories (NSAIDs) such as Aleve and Advil. I took them for other injuries over the years, but I knew that I could not take NSAIDs forever. I believe they are damaging to the body, especially with prolonged use. One natural alternative is turmeric. I used an organic, food-based product called Zyflammend, a natural anti-inflammatory, and it did wonders for me. Look for natural anti-inflammatory supplements and follow an anti-inflammatory diet—no nightshades, wheat, soy, etc.. White willow bark is also a wonderful natural alternative that reduces pain.

### A Case for the Use of Medical Marijuana

Although at the time I did not know about using medical marijuana to help heal my back, studies of how medical marijuana reduces pain and muscle spasticity are solid. There are cases where pain is ongoing and not relieved through conventional measures. Chronic pain and spasm have their own destructive patterns and damage on the mind, body, and spirit. I leave it up to the readers to decide what is best for them, but given the alternatives, I see no downside in assisting healing with a plant-based therapy, especially during such a challenging time as healing a back injury, versus potentially damaging and addictive pharmaceutical pain relievers. High quality medical marijuana tinctures are now more available to save your precious running lungs.

**Minerals**
What are bones and muscles made of? Minerals. To heal the body, the low back in particular, it needs ready access to support materials. The muscles and joints also need the right ratio of minerals to properly heal and maintain healthy function. I believe that you need to supplement your diet with minerals, even if you are eating a grass-fed, organic diet (which I do). The soil from which the animals are fed and the plants grown are probably deficient in minerals. Given the United States history of non-sustainable, supportive agricultural practices in the past century, it makes sense. Take an organic mineral and trace mineral supplement from a company such as New Chapter.

**Gentle Cleansing**
During the time of my recovery, I would fast on home cooked (home cooked only!) broths and herbal teas a few days a month. This nutrifies your body with minerals and collagen and brings your minds focus back to where it needs to be -

which is on healing. Break out Sally Fallon's book, *Nourishing Traditions*, or the GAPS Diet, by Natasha Campbell McBride, and find some broth and soup recipes that sound good to you!

**The Paleo or GAPS diet**

I think the healthiest way to eat is Paleo, Primal style or GAPS - which eliminates grains and most dairy (known to cause inflammation) from the diet. Between my naturopath, personal research, and ultimately my own experience, I have found it to be the best long-term diet for a life of fun running and a healthier, leaner body. Having been a vegetarian for well over a decade, I found my body recovers best from exercise with more lean animal proteins, healthy fats and lightly cooked vegetables and fermented foods vs. just vegetables and grains. The GAPS diet was designed to heal your gut. It may be just what your body needs. Try it for at least six weeks, and see if you feel better!

**Time Reframing**

In the grand scheme of things, three months, six months, or even a year is not that long - given that most people live at least seventy years. When you are injured, time slows down, and you can feel like healing is taking forever. If you have to change your ways for a short time, it's worth it, even if that short time is a few months. Focus on this! Do what it takes, right now, to make it work, and I promise you, you will be rewarded with run after joyous run for years to come!

**Disc Healing**
The healing process of the bulged disc required much more work and practice at stabilization. Running, as you have probably been told, is the worst thing for a bulged disc. The vertical force, subtle twisting, and bouncing challenge a disc that is not in optimal condition, so healing it takes patience and practicality. For me, the pain of the disc injury superseded the fracture, and healing took about a year.

While a disc heals, you want to rebuild the disc integrity, and you want to create the space between the vertebrae for it to comfortably exist. Disc integrity is helped with excellent nutrition, rest and supplements. Space is created by physically rebalancing the body. This is a healing symbiosis. Doing gentle work on a rebounder can ease your body into the feeling of running again, as well as massage your discs and joints. I highly recommend making the rebounder a part of your exercise regimen.

**Bone Healing**
Give the bones their time to heal with a brace, pins, or whatever solution you are working with. Obviously you want to avoid falling and trauma-inducing activities for at least a year to minimize your chance of a re-break. Look to a diet rich in bone broths to help your body heal faster. As a general rule, bones start to knit immediately and should be healed within three months. If you have pain beyond three months, something is not right.

**Walking: The Gateway Drug to Running**
If you can walk, do it. I know it is a far cry from running, but it gets you out and keeps your muscles in motion. Hiking is better, but grades both up and down can be problematic. Until you are pain-free, level walking is best and will probably be recommended by your treatment team. Trails offer lower impact than walking on pavement. The treadmill is also a great, low-impact part of your recovery program. How much walking you do depends on your pain levels and ability to maintain progress without offsetting your gains in flexibility and strength. Work with your physical therapist, and assess how your body feels during and after your walks.

**Pilates: The Mind and Muscle as One**
Pilates was key to helping my back to heal. Find a qualified Pilates instructor who is familiar with injury treatment, and schedule some individual sessions. If she is good, she will have a reformer and other crazy-looking props to help you learn how to realign your body. She will also teach you how to work from your core, which will stabilize and strengthen your low back forever. The majority of low-back injuries are the result of core imbalance and weakness. As you begin to strengthen your core, you will understand what it feels like and never forget it. This will also amplify your running potential!

**Run within Your Pain Tolerance**
The most critical time in getting back to running is the first

few months. The general rule is to run within your pain tolerance. As mentioned earlier, this can be tricky for those of us who ignore pain, but this is when you get to act like a baby and honor your pain. It's better to under-do than over-do. The goal is to have zero pain during or after.

# The First Run Back

*"If this moment truly matters to you, you will experience it fully"*
Deepak Chopra

Before I knew what I know now, my first attempted run after bulging my disc was wrought with tears and frustration. I should have started a lot slower and built from a foundation of comfort, but I was too impatient. Had I known about the lumbar brace that I later used for my fracture, I would have used it for those first few months of running. The lumbar brace creates more vertical expansion upward, and relieves pressure on the disc better than the narrower, SI-style brace. It also limits lumbar shearing and torsion movement. Talk to your physical therapist about using a lumbar brace, and find something that can be tailored to your injury.

In addition, use your rebounder before your first run and slowly introduce gentle bouncing to re-engage the discs shock absorbing qualities. This is a really fun , low impact way to get your body back to the feeling of running without the impact.

**WARNING:** months of work were ruined each time I ran prematurely, ran too long, or to intensely and because I thought I was healed. The run would be pain free, the after run not so much. Or maybe the run wasn't pain free and I did it anyway. Do not make this mistake. My criteria for a successful first run back are detailed below.

**Pre-Run Requirement**

When recovering from a low back injury, you can't jump in at a your race pace right off the bat - once you are cleared to run. You want to reengage slowly; gradually build time at your pain-free pace, add endurance to that pace, and then add speed. Time is the first running goal, speed always comes last.

To get ready to run again, your fitness and pain levels need to be in a stable place to take on the added stress of running. Everyones body is different when it comes to pain, but being pain free for about a month is probably a good rule of thumb. This allows you to have life happen and see how your back does within those circumstances.

**My criteria to advance on to running:**

1. Able to power-walk for at least 30 minutes everyday for several weeks in a row, pain free. Stride is powerful with hips behind you. Pain-free during and after these walks with no adverse reactions, spasticity, or splinting.

2. Able to consistently lift weights for a few sets with your arms, at least 10 pounds each.

3. Able to do consistently reasonable bouncing on the rebounder without pain or negative repercussions - at least 10 minute sessions.

## Transitioning to Running

Okay, you have met the above criteria - the day has come to run again! On your next walk, start by taking a few running strides on level ground. If this at all feels painful or weird, stop. Wait another week and try again. If those few running strides felt okay, go for fifteen seconds at a slow pace, stop, and continue with your walk. You are done running for the day. That's it, just 15 seconds. See how you feel later, you should have no additional pain or tightness. Now try this schedule: running 15 seconds every other day or every third day. This is best done on a treadmill, which has excellent shock-absorbing qualities. It also could be done on a track that has a cushiony surface. Commit to this schedule for a week, and see how your body feels - both during and after. I know it sounds like you are doing nothing and may even feel like you are doing nothing. But the purpose here is to re-introduce your body to running. This isn't about fitness, it's about helping your body re-adapt in the fastest way possible, which ironically means taking it slow at this point.

A common thing that happens, is that the run feels okay, but afterward your back doesn't feel great. The only way to not overdo, is to do a little at a time, wait (overnight), see how you feel, then do a little more. You have to understand that the run you do for 15 seconds you will feel 8 hours later.

**In summary:**

1. Be able to walk pain free every day for at least 30 minutes at a time for several weeks.

2. Attempt your first running stride for 15 seconds, then stop running for that day and continue your walk. See how you feel that evening.

3. Only walk the next day

4. The next day do the 15 seconds of running, and continue your walk. You should only be adding the running aspect of your walk every other day , or maybe even every third day, while walking every day. Your back should be feeling fine.

5. If your back is not feeling fine. Go back to just walking for another week. You are not ready yet.

It is important to not base your progress on one or two days - better to see how the week goes. The running stress is cumulative, so say to yourself: "I am at the 15 second easy running level for this week." Commit to that. If it all feels great, that is awesome, but still wait to see how you feel for that entire week. Take the weekend off from running. If at any time you are in pain or your back increases in muscle tightness, back off for a few days, and commit to another week at that previous level. If you have no pain or increased splinting, run 15 seconds at a slow pace, walk for 10 minutes, run another 15 seconds at a slow pace—and that's it for the running. Space the running this way to give your body a chance to adjust. Take it slow. There is no rush. Do that series twice and continue your walk. See how you feel at the end of the day.

Commit to a week of running at this level. If you feel pain during or after, go back to the previous level, in this case it would be walking, and say 1 day of running. Give that a go for another week. Stay at this level for 2 weeks. If all is going well, then try running for 30 seconds, walking for 10 minutes, and running for another 30 seconds.

**In summary, the pattern - run, walk, run:**
**30 seconds easy running, 10 minutes walking, 30 seconds easy running.**

In general, I recommend staying at each level for 2 weeks. This allows for several things to happen: gentle adaptation, days you don't feel great, or your schedule changes. You want to see how your body does under a variety conditions. So apply this recipe to your life over two weeks time and you will see how your body does. Ironically, the worst thing is to have two rock star days of running, then base all of your workout around that level, only to realized you have overdone and you are back to square one. It is best to "average". Let your body adapt to more difficult situations – then ask it to up level.

When you are ready, build up to 1 minute of running , followed by 10 minutes walking and 1 minute of running, all the while maintaining awareness of how you feel during and after. If you feel uncomfortable, go back to the previous level after a two-day break. There will be plateaus in your improvement, and this is normal. You may be at the one-minute level for three weeks, and that's okay. As long as your pain and splinting are kept in check, you are on the right track. If running every other day is too much, try every third day. Tailor your activity to your pain threshold and muscle activity, and be patient, patient, patient. Gradually extend your running time along this pattern;  run 2 minutes, walk 10 minutes.... then 3, then 4 etc... until you are back running at your normal level.

I cannot stress enough the importance of taking it slow for those first few weeks of running. The urge to break out and run like a gazelle may be strong, but doing so can set you back weeks, if not months. Remember your other exercise outlets, and be patient with yourself. Focus on the ultimate goal of running without pain. At this point, running should not be seen as fitness, but more of, "I am learning how to run again". This way your true fitness needs will be met with *other* exercise, and your running will just be seen as a new skill. It will take the pressure off.

## Conclusion

Running is one of the most challenging physical activities to return to after a low-back injury, and reclaiming your regular running routine can take time. But it is possible to make that time as short as possible when you follow a logical approach to healing. Be patient with yourself, and know, that if you follow a solid healing plan, you will get there.

Printed in Great Britain
by Amazon.co.uk, Ltd.,
Marston Gate.